The Tragedy of Mariam: The Fair Queen of Jewry

Lady Elizabeth Cary

THE TRAGEDIE OF MARIAM, THE FAIRE
Queene of Jewry.

Written by that learned,
vertuous, and truly noble Ladie,
Elizabeth Cary

1613.

TO DIANAES
EARTHLIE DEPUTESSE,
and my worthy Sister, Mistris
Elizabeth Carye.

WHen cheerfull *Phœbus* his full course hath run,
His sisters fainter beams our harts doth cheere:
So your faire Brother is to mee the Sunne,
And you his Sister as my Moone appeare.

You are my next belov'd, my second Friend,
For when my *Phœbus* absence makes it Night,
Whilst to th' *Antipodes* his beames do bend,
From you my *Phœbe*, shines my second Light.

Hee like to *SOL*, cleare-sighted, constant, free,
You *LUNA*-like, unspotted, chast, divine:
Hee shone on *Sicily*, you destin'd bee,
T'illumine the now obscurde *Palestine*.
My first was consecrated to *Apollo*,
My second to *DIANA* now shall follow.

E.C.

The names of the Speakers.

Herod, King of Judea.

Doris, his first Wife.

Mariam, his second Wife.

Salome, Herods Sister.

Antipater his sonne by Salome.

Alexandra, Mariams mother.

Sillius, Prince of Arabia.

Constabarus, husband to Salome.

Pheroras, Herods Brother.

Graphina, his Love.

Babus first Sonne.

Babus second Sonne.

Annanell, the high Priest.

Sohemus, a Counseller to Herod.

Nuntio.

Bu, another Messenger.

Chorus, a Companie of Jewes.

The Argument.

HErod the sonne of *Antipater*, (an *Idumean*,) having crept by the favor of the *Romanes*, into the Jewish Monarchie, married *Mariam* the daughter of *Hircanus*, the rightfull *King and Priest*, and for her (besides her high blood, being of singular beautie) hee reputiated *Doris*, his former Wife, by whome hee had Children.

This *Mariam* had a Brother called *Aristobolus*, and next him and *Hircanus* his Graund-father, *Herod* in his Wife's right had the best title. Therefore to remoove them, he charged the first with treason: and put him to death; and drowned the second under colour of sport. *Alexandra*, Daughter to the one, and Mother to the other, accused him for their deaths before *Anthony*.

So when hee was forc'te to goe answere this Accusation at *Rome*, he left the custodie of his wife to *Josephus* his Uncle, that had married his Sister *Salome*, and out of a violent affection (unwilling any should enjoy her after him) hee gave strict and private commaundement, that if hee were slaine, shee should be put to death. But he returned with much honour, yet found his Wife extreamely discontented, to whom *Josephus* had (meaning it for the best, to prove *Herod* loved her) revealed his charge.

So by *Salomes* accusation hee put *Josephus* to death, but was reconciled to *Mariam*, who still bare the death of her Friends exceeding hardly.

In this meane time *Herod* was againe necessarily to revisite *Rome*, for *Cæsar* having overthrowne *Anthony* his great friend, was likely to make an alteration of his Fortune.

In his absence, newes came to *Jerusalem* that *Cæsar* had put him to death, their willingnes it should be so, together with the likelyhood, gave this Rumor so good credit, as *Sohemus* that had suceeded *Josephus* charge, succeeded him likewise in revealing it. So at *Herods* returne which was speedy and unexpected, he found *Mariam* so farre from joye, that she shewed apparent signes of sorrow. Hee still desiring to winne her to a better humour, she being very unable to conceale her passion, fell to upbraiding him with her Brothers death. As they were thus debating, came in a fellow with a Cuppe of Wine, who hired by *Salome*, saide first, it was a Love potion, which *Mariam* desired to deliver to the King: but afterwards he affirmed that it was a poyson, and that *Sohemus* had tolde her somewhat, which procured the vehement hate in her.

The King hearing this, more moved with Jealousie of *Sohemus*, then with this intent of poyson, sent her away, and presently after by the instigation of *Salome*, she was beheaded. Which rashnes was afterward punished in him, with an intollerable and almost Frantike passion for her death.

[handwritten: Mariam was part of the chorus]

The Tragedy of Mariam: The Fair Queen of Jewry

Actus 1. Scœna 1

Mariam sola. → *[handwritten: Just heard her (hated) husband has died]*

[handwritten left margin: rare for a woman to talk this much]

[handwritten right: inner relief / outer grief]

HOw oft have I with publike voyce runne on?
To censure *Romes* last *Hero* for deceit:
Because he wept when *Pompeis* life was gone,
Yet when he liv'd, hee thought his Name too great.
But now I doe recant, and *Roman* Lord
Excuse too rash a judgement in a woman:
My Sexe pleads pardon, pardon then afford,
Mistaking is with us, but too too common.

[handwritten right: Chorus / Was / Silent ↓ / Womens Role.]

Now doe I finde by selfe Experience taught,
One Object yeelds both griefe and joy:
You wept indeed, when on his worth you thought,
But joyd that slaughter did your Foe destroy.
So at his death your Eyes true droppes did raine,
Whom dead, you did not wish alive againe.
When *Herod* liv'd, that now is done to death,
Oft have I wisht that I from him were free:
Oft have I wisht that he might lose his breath,
Oft have I wisht his Carkas dead to see.
Then Rage and Scorne had put my love to flight,
That Love which once on him was firmely set:
Hate hid his true affection from my sight,
And kept my heart from paying him his debt.
And blame me not, for *Herods* Jealousie
Had power even constancie itselfe to change:
For hee by barring me from libertie,
To shunne my ranging, taught me first to range.
But yet too chast a Scholler was my hart,
To learn to love another then my Lord:
To leave his Love, my lessons former part,

I quickly learn'd, the other I abhord.
But now his death to memorie doth call,
The tender love, that he to *Mariam* bare:

1

And mine to him, this makes those rivers fall,
Which by an other thought unmoistned are.
For *Aristobolus* the lowlyest youth
That ever did in Angels shape appeare:
The cruell *Herod* was not mov'd to ruth,
Then why grieves *Mariam Herods* death to heare?
Why joy I not the tongue no more shall speake,
That yeelded forth my brothers latest dome:
Both youth and beautie might thy furie breake,
And both in him did ill befit a Tombe.
And worthy Grandsire ill did he requite,
His high Assent alone by thee procur'd,
Except he murdred thee to free the spright
Which still he thought on earth too long immur'd.
How happie was it that *Sohemus* maide [minde]
Was mov'd to pittie my distrest estate?
Might *Herods* life a trustie servant finde,
My death to his had bene unseparate.
These thoughts have power, his death to make me beare,
Nay more, to wish the newes may firmely hold:
Yet cannot this repulse some falling teare,
That will against my will some griefe unfold.
And more I owe him for his love to me,
The deepest love that ever yet was seene:
Yet had I rather much a milke-maide bee,
Then be the Monarke of *Judeas* Queene.
It was for nought but love, he wisht his end
Might to my death but the vaunt-currier prove:
But I had rather still be foe then friend,
To him that saves for hate, and kills for love.
Hard-hearted *Mariam*, at thy discontent,
What flouds of teares have drencht his manly face?
How canst thou then so faintly now lament,
Thy truest lovers death, a deaths disgrace:
I, now mine eyes you do begin to right

The wrongs of your admirer. And my Lord,
Long since you should have put your smiles to flight,

Ill doth a widowed eye with joy accord,
Why now me thinkes the love I bare him then,
When virgin freedome left me unrestraind:
Doth to my heart begin to creepe agen,
My passion now is far from being faind,
But teares flie backe, and hide you in your bankes,
You must not be to *Alexandra* seene:
For if my mone be spide, but little thankes
Shall *Mariam* have, from that incensed Queene.

Actus 1: Scœna 2.

Mariam. Alexandra.

Alex:

WHat meanes these teares? My *Mariam* doth mistake,
The newes we heard did tell the *Tyrants* end:
What weepst thou for thy brothers murthers sake,
Will ever wight a teare for *Herod* spend?
My curse pursue his breathless trunke and spirit,
Base *Edomite* the damned *Esaus* heire:
Must he ere *Jacobs* child the crowne inherit?
Must he vile wretch be set in *Davids* chaire?
No *Davids* soule within the bosome plac'te,
Of our forefather *Abram* was asham'd:
To see his seat with such a toade disgrac'te,
That seat that hath by *Judas* race bene fain'd.
Thou fatall enemie to royall blood,
Did not the murther of my boy suffice,
To stop thy cruell mouth that gaping stood?
But must thou dim the mild *Hircanus* eyes? → Mariam's dad
My gratious father, whose too readie hand
Did lift this *Idumean* from the dust:
And he ungratefull catiffe did withstand,
The man that did in him most friendly trust.

3

What kingdomes right could cruell *Herod* claime,
Was he not *Esaus* Issue, heyre of hell?
Then what succession can he have but shame?
Did not his Ancestor his birth-right sell? ——

in Mariam's face.

O yes, he doth from *Edoms* name derive,
His cruell nature which with blood is fed:
That made him me of Sire and sonne deprive,
He ever thirsts for blood, and blood is red.
Weepst thou because his love to thee was bent?
And readst thou love in crimson caracters?
Slew he thy friends to worke thy hearts content?
No: hate may justly call that action hers.
He gave the sacred Priesthood for thy sake,
To *Aristobolus*. Yet doomde him dead:
Before his backe the *Ephod* warme could make,
And ere the *Myter* setled on his head,
Oh had he given my boy no lesse then right,
The double oyle should to his forehead bring:
A double honour, shining doubly bright,
His birth annoynted him both Priest and King.
And say my father, and my sonne he slewe,
To royalize by right your Prince borne breath:
Was love the cause, can *Mariam* deeme it true,
That *Mariam* gave commandment for her death?
I know by fits, he shewd some signes of love,
And yet not love, but raging lunacie:
And this his hate to thee may justly prove,
That sure he hates *Hercanus* familie.
Who knowes if he unconstant wavering Lord,
His love to *Doris* had renew'd againe?
And that he might his bed to her afford,
Perchance he wisht that *Mariam* might be slaine.

Nun. [*Mariam.*] *Doris,* Alas her time of love was past,
Those coales were rakte in embers long agoe;
If *Mariams* love and she was now disgrast,
Nor did I glorie in her overthrowe.

Plop of Herod on Stage.

Shows he is a constant within the play.

4

He not a whit his first borne sonne esteem'd,
Because as well as his he was not mine.
My children onely for his owne he deem'd,
These boyes that did descend from royall line.
These did he stile his heyres to *Davids* throne,
My *Alexander* if he live, shall sit

In the Majesticke seat of *Salamon.*
To will it so, did *Herod* thinke it fit.

Alex. Why? who can claime from *Alexanders* brood
That Gold adorned Lyon-guarded Chaire?
Was *Alexander* not of *Davids* blood?
And was not *Mariam Alexanders* heire?
What more then right could *Herod* then bestow,
And who will thinke except for more then right,
He did not raise them, for they were not low,
But borne to weare the Crowne in his despight:
Then send those teares away that are not sent
To thee by season, but by passions power:
Thine eyes to cheere, thy cheekes to smiles be bent,
And entertaine with joy this happy houre.
Felicitie, if when shee comes, she findes
A mourning habite, and a cheerless looke,
Will thinke she is not welcome to thy minde,
And so perchance her lodging will not brooke.
Oh keepe her whilest thou hast her, if she goe
She will not easily returne againe:
Full many a yeere have I indur'd in woe,
Yet still have sude her presence to obtaine:
And did not I to her as presents send
A Table, that best Art did beautifie
Of two, to whom Heaven did best feature lend,
To woe her love by winning *Anthony*
For when a Princes favour we doe crave,
We first their Mynions loves do seeke to winne:
So I, that sought Felicitie to have,
Did with her Mynion *Anthony* beginne,

5

With double flight I sought to captivate
The warlike lover, but I did not right:
For if my gift had borne but halfe the rate,
The *Roman* had beene over-taken quite.
But now he fared like a hungry guest,
That to some plenteous festivall is gone,
Now this, now that, hee deems to eate were best,
Such choice doth make him let them all alone.

The boyes large forehead first did fayrest seeme
Then glaunst his eye upon my *Mariams* cheeke:
And that without comparison did deeme,
What was in eyther but he most did leeke.
And thus distracted, eythers beauties might
Within the others excellence was drown'd:
Too much delight did bare him from delight,
For eithers love, the others did confound.
Where if thy portraiture had onely gone,
His life from *Herod*, *Anthony* had taken:
He would have loved thee, and thee alone,
And left the browne *Egyptian* cleane forsaken.
And *Cleopatra* then to seeke had bene,
So firme a lover of her wayned face:
Then great *Anthonius* fall we had not seene,
By her that fled to have him hold the chase.
Then *Mariam* in a *Romans* Chariot set,
In place of *Cleopatra* might have showne:
A mart of Beauties in her visage met,
And part in this, that they were all her owne.

Ma. Not to be Emprise of aspiring *Rome*,
Would *Mariam* like to *Cleopatra* live:
With purest body will I presse my Toome,
And wish no favours *Anthony* could give.

Alex. Let us retire us, that we may resolve
How now to deale in this reversed state:

6

Great are th'affaires that we must now revolve,
And great affaires must not be taken late.

Actus 1. Scœna 3.

Mariam. Alexandra. Salome.

Salome.

MOre plotting yet? Why? now you have the thing
For which so oft you spent your supliant breath:
And *Mariam* hopes to have another King,
Her eyes doe sparkle joy for *Herods* death.

Alex. If she desir'd another King to have,
She might before she came in *Herods* bed
Have had her wish. More Kings then one did crave,
For leave to set a Crowne upon her head.
I think with more then reason she laments,
That she is freed from such a sad annoy:
Who ist will weepe to part from discontent,
And if she joy, she did not causelesse joy.

Sal. You durst not thus have given your tongue the raine,
If noble *Herod* still remaind in life:
Your daughters betters farre I dare maintaine,
Might have rejoyc'd to be my brothers wife.

Mar. My betters farre, base woman t'is untrue,
You scarce have ever my superiors seene:
For *Mariams* servants were as good as you,
Before she came to be *Judeas* Queene.

Sal. Now stirs the tongue that is so quickly mov'd,
But more then once your collor have I borne:

Your fumish words are sooner sayd then prov'd,
And *Salomes* reply is onely scorne.

Mar. Scorne those that are for thy companions held,
Though I thy brothers face had never seene,
My birth thy baser birth so farre exceld,
I had to both of you the Princesse bene.
Thou party Jew, and party Edomite,
Thou Mongrell: issu'd from rejected race,
Thy Ancestors against the Heavens did fight,
And thou like them wilt heavenly birth disgrace.

Sal. Still twit you me with nothing but my birth,
What ods betwixt your ancestors and mine?
Both borne of *Adam*, both were made of Earth,
And both did come from holy *Abrahams* line.

Mar. I favour thee when nothing else *I* say,
With thy blacke acts ile not pollute my breath:
Else to thy charge *I* might full justly lay
A shamefull life, besides a husbands death.

Sal. Tis true indeed, *I* did the plots reveale,
That past betwixt your favorites and you:
I ment not *I*, a traytor to conceale.

Thus *Salome* your Mynion *Joseph* slue.

Mar. Heaven, dost thou meane this Infamy to smother?
Let slandred *Mariam* ope thy closed eare:
Selfe guilt hath ever bene suspitious mother,
And therefore I this speech with patience beare.
No, had not *Salomes* unstedfast heart,
In *Josephus* stead her *Constabarus* plast
To free her selfe, she had not usde the art,
To slander haplesse *Mariam* for unchast.

Alex. Come *Mariam*, let us goe: it is no boote
To let the head contend against the foote.

Actus 1. Scœna 4.

Salome, Sola.

Soliloquy [handwritten annotation]

LIves *Salome*, to get so base a stile
As foote, to the proud *Mariam Herods* spirit?
In happy time for her endured exile,
For did he live she should not misse her merit:
But he is dead: and though he were my Brother,
His death such store of Cinders cannot cast
My Coales of love to quench: for though they smother
The flames a while, yet will they out at last.
Oh blest *Arabia*, in best climate plast,
I by the Fruit will censure of the Tree:
Tis not in vaine, thy happy name thou hast,
If all *Arabians* like *Silleus* bee:
Had not my Fate bene too too contrary,
When I on *Constabarus* first did gaze,
Silleus had beene object to mine eye:
Whose lookes and personage must allyes amaze.
But now ill Fated *Salome*, thy tongue
To *Constabarus* by itselfe is tide:
And now except I doe the Ebrew wrong
I cannot be the faire *Arabian* Bride:
What childish lets are these? Why stand I now
On honourable points? Tis long agoe

Since shame was written on my tainted brow,
And certaine tis, that shame is honours foe.
Had I upon my reputation stood,
Had I affected an unspotted life,
Josephus vaines had still bene stuft with blood,
And I to him had liv'd a sober wife.

9

The Tragedy of Mariam: The Fair Queen of Jewry

Then had I never cast an eye of love,
On *Constabarus* now detested face,
Then had I kept my thoughts without remouve
And blusht at motion of the least disgrace:
But shame is gone, and honour wipt away,
And Impudencie on my forehead fits:
She bids me worke my will without delay,
And for my will I will imploy my wits.
He loves, I love; what then can be the cause,
Keepes me for being the *Arabians* wife?
It is the principles of *Moses* lawes,
For *Constabarus* still remaines in life,
If he to me did beare as Earnest hate,
As I to him, for him there were an ease,
A separating bill might free his fate:
From such a yoke that did so much displease.
Why should such priviledge to man be given?
Or given to them, why bard from women then?
Are men then we in greater grace with Heaven?
Or cannot women hate as well as men?
He be the custome-breaker: and beginne
To shew my Sexe the way to freedomes doore,
And with an offring will I purge my sinne,
The lawe was made for none but who are poore.
If *Herod* had liv'd, I might to him accuse
My present Lord, But for the futures sake
Then would I tell the King he did refuse
The sonnes of *Baba* in his power to take.
But now I must divorce him from my bed,
That my *Silleus* may possesse his roome:
Had I not begd his life he had bene dead,
I curse my tongue the hindrer of his doome,

But then my wandring hearte to him was fast,
Nor did *I* dreame of chaunge: *Silleus* said,
He would be here, and see he comes at last,
Had *I* not nam'd him longer had he staid.

Actus 1. Sœna 5.

Salome, Silleus.

Silleus. WEll found faire *Salome Judeas* pride,
Hath thy innated wisedome found the way
To make *Silleus* deeme him deified,
By gaining thee a more then precious pray?

Salo. I have devisde the best I can devise,
A more imperfect meanes was never found:
But what cares *Salome*, it doth suffice
If our indevours with their end be crown'd.
In this our land we have an ancient use,
Permitted first by our law-givers head:
Who hates his wife, though for no just abuse,
May with a bill divorce her from his bed.
But in this custom women are not free,
Yet I for once will wrest it, blame not thou
The ill I doe, since what I do'es for thee,
Though others blame, *Silleus* should allow.

Silleus. Thinkes *Salome*, *Silleus* hath a tongue
To censure her faire actions: let my blood
Bedash my proper brow, for such a wrong,
The being yours, can make even vices good:
Arabia joy, prepare thy earth with greene,
Thou never happie wert indeed till now:
Now shall thy ground be trod by beauties Queene,
Her foote is destin'd to depresse thy brow.
Thou shalt faire *Salome* command as much
As if the royall ornament were thine:
The weaknes of *Arabias* King is such,
The kingdome is not his so much as mine.
My mouth is our *Obodas* oracle,
Who thinkes not ought but what *Silleus* will?

And thou rare creature, *Asias* miracle,
Shalt be to me as its *Obodas* still.

Salome. Tis not for glory *I* thy love accept,
Judea yeelds me honours worthy store:
Had not affection in my bosome crept,
My native country should my life deplore.
Were not *Silleus* he with home I goe,
I would not change my *Palestine* for *Rome*:
Much lesse would I a glorious state to shew,
Goe far to purchase an *Arabian* toome.

Silleus. Far be it from *Silleus* so to thinke,
I know it is thy gratitude requites
The love that is in me, and shall not shrinke
Till death doe sever me from earths delights.

Salom. But whist; me thinkes the wolfe is in our talke,
Be gone *Silleus*, who doth here arrive?
Tis *Constabarus* that doth hither walke,
Ile find a quarrell, him from me to drive.

Sille. Farewell, but were it not for thy commaund,
In his despight *Silleus* here would stand.

Actus 1: Sœna 6.

←——— *Salome. Constabarus.*

Const. OH *Salome*, how much you wrõg your name,
Your race, your country, and your husband most?
A straungers private conference is shame,
I blush for you, that have your blushing lost.
Oft have I found, and found you to my griefe,
Consorted with this base *Arabian* heere:
Heaven knowes that you have bin my comfort chiefe,

12

Then doe not now my greater plague appeare.
Now by the stately Carved edifice
That on Mount *Sion* makes so faire a show,
And by the Altar fit for sacrifice,
I love thee more then thou thy selfe doest know.
Oft with a silent sorrow have I heard
How ill *Judeas* mouth doth censure thee:

And did I not thine honour much regard,
Thou shouldst not be exhorted thus for mee.
Didst thou but know the worth of honest fame,
How much a vertuous woman is esteem'd,
Thou wouldest like hell eschew deserved shame,
And seeke to be both chast and chastly deem'd.
Our wisest Prince did say, and true he said,
A vertuous woman crownes her husbands head.

Salome. Did I for this, upreare thy lowe estate?
Did I for this requitall begge thy life,
That thou hadst forfeited haples fate?
To be to such a thankles wretch the wife.
This hand of mine hath lifted up thy head,
Which many a day agoe had falne full lowe,
Because the sonnes of *Baba* are not dead,
To me thou doest both life and fortune owe.

Const. You have my patience often exercisde,
Use make my choller keepe within the bankes:
Yet boast no more, but be by me advisde,
A benefit upbraided, forfeits thankes:
I prethy *Salome* dismisse this mood,
Thou doest not know how ill it fits thy place:
My words were all intended for thy good,
To raise thine honour and to stop disgrace.

Sa. To stop disgrace? take thou no care for mee,
Nay do thy worst, thy worst I set not by:
No shame of mine is like to light on thee,

13

Thy love and admonitions I defie.
Thou shalt no hower longer call me wife,
Thy jealousie procures my hate so deepe:
That I from thee doe meane to free my life,
By a divorcing bill before I sleepe.

Const. Are Hebrew women now transform'd to men?
Why do you not as well our battels fight,
And weare our armour? Suffer this, and then
Let all the world be topsie turved quite.
Let fishes graze, beastes, swine, and birds descend,
Let fire burne downewards whilst the earth aspires:

Let Winters heat and Summers cold offend,
Let Thistels growe on Vines, and Grapes on Briers,
Set us to Spinne or Sowe, or at the best
Make us Wood-hewers, Waters-bearing wights:
For sacred service let us take no rest,
Use us as *Joshua* did the *Gibonites.*

Salom. Hold on your talke, till it be time to end,
For me I am resolv'd it shall be so:
Though I be first that to this course do bend,
I shall not be the last full well *I* know.

Const. Why then be witnesse Heav'n, the Judge of sinnes,
Be witnesse Spirits that eschew the darke:
Be witnesse Angels, witnesse Cherubins,
Whose semblance fits upon the holy Arke:
Be witnesse earth, be witnesse *Palestine,*
Be witnesse *Davids* Citie, if my heart
Did ever merit such an act of thine:
Or if the fault be mine that make us part,
Since mildest *Moses* friend unto the Lord,
Did worke his wonders in the land of *Ham,*
And slew the first-borne Babes without a sword,
In signe whereof we eate the holy Lambe:
Till now that fourteene hundred yeeres are past,

14

Since first the Law with us hath been in force:
You are the first, and will I hope, be last,
That ever sought her husband to divorce.

Salom. I meane not to be led by president,
My will shall be to me in stead of Law.

*liberated
free speaking*

Const. I feare me much you will too late repent,
That you have ever liv'd so void of awe:
This is *Silleus* love that makes you thus
Reverse all order: you must next be his.
But if my thoughts aright the cause discusse,
In winning you, he gaines no lasting blisse,
I was *Silleus,* and not long agoe
Josephus then was *Constabarus* now:
When you became my friend you prov'd his foe,
As now for him you breake to me your vowd.

Sal. If once I lov'd you, greater is your debt:
For certaine tis that you deserved it not. ———>   *didn't deserve
her love!*
And undeserved love we soone forget,
And therefore that to me can be no blot.
But now fare ill my once beloved Lord,
Yet never more belov'd then now abhord.

(exit)

Const. Yet *Constabarus* biddeth thee farewell.
Farewell light creature. Heaven forgive thy sinne:
My prophecying spirit doth foretell
Thy wavering thoughts doe yet but new beginne,
Yet I have better scap'd then *Joseph* did,
But if our *Herods* death had bene delayd,
The valiant youths that I so long have hid,
Had bene by her, and I for them betrayd.
Therefore in happy houre did *Cæsar* give
The fatall blow to wanton *Anthony.*
For had he lived, our *Herod* then should live,
But great *Anthonius* death made *Herod* dye.
Had he enjoyed his breath, not I alone

Had beene in danger of a deadly fall:
But *Mariam* had the way of perill gone,
Though by the Tyrant most belov'd of all.
The sweet fac'd *Mariam* as free from guilt
As Heaven from spots, yet had her Lord come backe
Her purest blood had bene unjustly spilt,
And *Salome* it was would worke her wracke.
Though all *Judea* yeeld her innocent,
She often hath bene neere to punishment.

Chorus.

THose mindes that wholy dote upon delight,
Except they onely joy in inward good,
Still hope at last to hop upon the right,
And so from Sand they leape in loathsome mud.
Fond wretches, seeking what they cannot finde,
For no content attends a wavering minde.
If wealth they doe desire, and wealth attaine,

Then wondrous faine would they to honor lep:
Of meane degree they doe in honor gaine,
They would but wish a little higher step.
Thus step to step, and wealth to wealth they ad,
Yet cannot all their plenty make them glad.

Yet oft we see that some in humble state,
Are chreefull, pleasant, happy, and content:
When those indeed that are of higher state,
With vaine additions do their thoughts torment.
Th'one would to his minde his fortune binde,
T'hother to his fortune frames his minde.

To with varietie is signe of griefe,
For if you like your state as now it is,
Why should an alteration bring reliefe?
Nay change would then be fear'd as losse of blis,

16

That man is onely happy in his Fate,
That is delighted in a setled state.

Still *Mariam* wisht she from her Lord were free,
For expectation of varietie:
Yet now she sees her wishes prosperous bee,
She grieves, because her Lord so soone did die.
Who can those vast imaginations feede,
Where in a propertie, contempt doth breede?

Were *Herod* now perchance to live againe,
She would againe as much be grieved at that:
All that she may, she ever doth disdaine,
Her wishes guide her to she knowes not what.
And sad must be their lookes, their honor sower,
That care for nothing being in their power.

Actus 2. Scœna 1.

Pheroras and Graphina.

Pher. T'Is true *Graphina*, now the time drawes nye
Wherin the holy Priest with hallowed right,

The happy long desired knot shall tie,
Pheroras and *Graphina* to unite;
How oft have I with lifted hands implor'd
This blessed houre, till now implord in vaine,
Which hath my wished libertie restor'd,
And made my subject selfe my owne againe,
Thy love faire Mayd upon mine eye doth sit,
Whose nature hot doth dry the moysture all,
Which were in nature, and in reason fit
For my monachall Brothers death to fall:
Had *Herod* liv'd, he would have pluckt my hand
From faire *Graphinas* Palme perforce: and tide
The same in hatefull and despised band,
For I had had a Baby to my Bride:
Scarce can her Infant tongue with easie voice
Her name distinguish to anothers care
Yet had he liv'd, his power, and not my choise
Had made me solembly the contract sweare.
Have I not cause in such a change to joy?
What? though she be my Neece, a Princesse borne,
Neere bloods without respect: high birth a toy.
Since Love can teach blood and kindreds scorne.
What booted it that he did raise my head,
To be his Realmes Copartner, Kingdomes mate,
Withall, he kept *Graphina* from my bed,
More wisht by me then thrice *Judeas* state.
Oh, could not he be skilful! Judge in love,
That doted upon his *Mariams* face?
He, for his passion, *Doris* did remove.
I needed not a lawfull Wife displace,

It could not be but he had power to judge,
But he that never grudg'd a Kingdomes share,
This well knowne happinesse to me did grudge:
And ment to be therein without compare.
Else had I bene his equall in loves hoast,
For though the Diadem on *Mariams* head
Corrupt the vulgar judgements, I will boast
Graphinas brow's as white, her cheekes as red.

Why speaks thou not faire creature? move thy tongue,
For Silence is a signe of discontent:
It were to both our loves too great a wrong
If now this hower do find thee sadly bent.

Graph. Mistake me not my Lord, too oft have I
Desir'd this time to come with winged feete,
To be inwrapt with griefe when tis too nie,
You know my wishes ever yours did meete:
If I be silent, tis no more but feare
That I should say too little when I speake:
But since you will my imperfections beare,
In spight of doubt I will my silence breake:
Yet might amazement tie my moving tongue,
But that I know before *Pheroras* minde,
I have admired your affection long:
And cannot yet therein a reason finde.
Your hand hath lifted me from lowest state,
To highest eminencie wondrous grace,
And me your hand-maid have you made your mate,
Though all but you alone doe count me base.
You have preserved me pure at my request,
Though you so weake a vassaile might constraine
To yeeld to your high will, then last not best
In my respect a Princesse you disdaine,
Then need not all these favours studie crave,
To be requited by a simple maide:
And studie still you know must silence have,
Then be my cause for silence justly waide,

But studie cannot boote nor I requite,
Except your lowly hand-maides steadfast love
And fast obedience may your mind delight,
I will not promise more then I can prove.

Phero. That studie needs not let *Graphina* smile,
And I desire no greater recompence:
I cannot vaunt me in a glorious stile,
Nor shew my love in far-fetcht eloquence:
But this beleeve me, never *Herods* heart
Hath held his Prince-borne beautie famed wife

In neerer place then thou faire virgin art,
To him that holds the glory of his life.
Should *Herods* body leave the Sepulcher,
And entertaine the sever'd ghost againe:
He should not be my nuptiall hinderer,
Except he hindred it with dying paine.
Come faire *Graphina*, let us goe in state,
This wish-indeered time to celebrate.

Actus 2. Scœna 2.

Constabarus and Babus Sonnes.

Babus. I. Sonne.

NOw valiant friend you have our lives redeem'd,
Which lives as sav'd by you, to you are due:
Command and you shall see your selfe esteem'd,
Our lives and liberties belong to you.
This twice six yeares with hazard of your life,
You have conceal'd us from the tyrants sword:
Though cruell *Herods* sister were your wife,
You durst in scorne of fear this grace afford.
In recompence we know not what to say,

A poore reward were thankes for such a merit,
Our truest friendship at your feete we lay,
The best requitall to a noble spirit.

Const. Oh how you wrong our friendship valiant youth,
With friends there is not such a word as det:
Where amitie is tide with bond of truth,
All benefits are there in common set,
Then is the golden age with them renew'd,
All names of properties are banisht quite:
Division, and distinction, are eschew'd:
Each hath to what belongs to others right.
And tis not sure so full a benefit,
Freely to give, as freely to require:
A bountious act hath glory following it,
They cause the glory that the act desire.

All friendship should the pattern imitate,
Of *Jesses* Sonne and valiant *Jonathan:*
For neither Soveraignes nor fathers hate,
A friendship fixt on vertue sever can.
Too much of this, tis written in the heart,
And need no amplifying with the tongue:
Now may you from your living tombe depart,
Where *Herods* life hath kept you overlong.
Too great an injury to a noble minde,
To be quicke buried, you had purchast fame,
Some yeares a goe, but that you were confinde.
While thousand meaner did advance their name.
Your best of life, the prime of all your yeares,
Your time of action is from you bereft.
Twelve winters have you overpast in feares:
Yet if you use it well, enough is left.
And who can doubt but you will use it well?
The sonnes of *Babus* have it by descent:
In all their thoughts each action to excell,
Boldly to act, and wisely to invent.

Babus 2. Sonne.

Had it not like the hatefull cuckoe beene,
Whose riper age his infant nurse doth kill:
So long we had not kept ourselves unseene,
But *Constabarus* safely crost our will:
For had the Tyrant fixt his cruell eye,
On our concealed faces wrath had swaide
His justice so, that he had forst us die.
And dearer price then life we should have paid,
For you our truest friend had falne with us:
And we much like a house on pillers set,
Had cleane deprest our prop, and therefore thus
Our readie will with our concealment met.
But now that you faire Lord are daungerlesse,
The Sonnes of *Baba* shall their rigor show:
And prove it was not basenes did oppresse
Our hearts so long, but honour kept them low.

Ba. 1. Sonne. Yet do I feare this tale of *Herods* death,
At last will prove a very tale indeed:

It gives me strongly in my minde, his breath
Will be preserv'd to make a number bleed:
I wish not therefore to be set at large,
Yet peril to my selfe I do not feare:
Let us for some daies longer be your charge,
Till we of *Herods* state the truth do heare.

Const. What art thou turn'd a coward noble youth,
That thou beginst to doubt, undoubted truth?

Babus. I. Son. Were it my brothers tongue that cast this doubt,
I fro his hart would have the question out:
With this keene fauchion, but tis you my Lord
Against whose head I must not lift a sword:
I am so tide in gratitude *Const.* believe
You have no cause to take it ill,

22

If any word of mine your heart did grieve,
The word discented from the speakers will,
I know it was not feare the doubt begun,
But rather valour and your care of me,
A coward could not be your fathers sonne,
Yet know I doubts unnecessarie be:
For who can thinke that in *Anthonius* fall,
Herod his bosome friend should scape unbrusde:
Then *Cæsar* we might thee an idiot call,
If thou by him should'st be so farre abusde.

Babus. 2. Sonne. Lord *Constab.* let me tell you this,
Upon submission *Cæsar* will forgive:
And therefore though the tyrant did amisse,
It may fall out that he will let him live.
Not many yeares agone it is since I
Directed thither by my fathers care,
In famous *Rome* for twice twelve monthes did live,
My life from *Hebrewes* crueltie to spare,
There though I were but yet of boyish age,
I bent mine eye to marke, mine eares to heare.
Where I did see *Octavious* then a page,
When first he did to *Julius* sight appeare:
Me thought *I* saw such mildnes in his face,
And such a sweetnes in his lookes did grow,

Withall, commixt with so majesticke grace,
His Phismony his Fortune did foreshow:
For this I am indebted to mine eye,
But then mine eare receiv'd more evidence,
By that I knew his love to clemency,
How he with hottest choller could dispence.

Const. But we have more then barely heard the news,
It hath bin twice confirm'd. And though some tongue
Might be so false, with false report t'abuse,
A false report hath never lasted long.
But be it so that *Herod* have his life,

Concealement would not then a whit availe:
For certaine t'is, that she that was my wife,
Would not to set her accusation faile.
And therefore now as good the venture give,
And free our selves from blot of cowardise:
As show a pittifull desire to live,
For, who can pittie but they must despise?

Babus first sonne.

I yeeld, but to necessitie I yeeld,
I dare upon this doubt ingage mine arme:
That *Herod* shall againe this kingdome weeld,
And prove his death to be a false alarme.

Babus second sonne.

I doubt it too: God grant it be an error,
Tis best without a cause to be in terror:
And rather had I, though my soule be mine,
My soule should lie, then prove a true divine.

Const. Come, come, let feare goe seeke a dastards nest,
Undaunted courage lies in a noble brest.

Actus 2. Scœna 3.

Doris and Antipater.

Dor. YOur royall buildings bow your loftie side,
And scope to her that is by right your Queen:

Let your humilitie upbraid the pride
Of those in whom no due respect is seene:
Nine times have we with Trumpets haughtie sound,
And banishing sow'r Leaven from our taste:

24

Observ'd the feast that takes the fruit from ground.
Since I faire Citie did behold thee last,
So long it is since *Mariams* purer cheeke
Did rob from mine the glory. And so long
Since I returnd my native Towne to seeke:
And with me nothing but the sence of wrong.
And thee my Boy, whose birth though great it were,
Yet have thy after fortunes prov'd but poore:
When thou wert borne how little did I feare
Thou shouldst be thrust from forth thy Fathers doore.
Art thout not *Herods* right begotten Sonne?
Was not the hapless *Doris*, *Herods* wife?
Yes: ere he had the Hebrew kingdome wonne,
I was companion to his private life.
Was *I* not faire enough to be a Queene?
Why ere thou wert to me false Monarch tide,
My lake of beauty might as well be seene,
As after *I* had liv'd five yeeres thy Bride.
Yet then thine oath came powring like the raine,
Which all affirm'd my face without compare:
And that if thou might'st *Doris* love obtaine,
For all the world besides thou didst not care.
Then was *I* yong, and rich, and nobly borne,
And therefore worthy to be *Herods* mate:
Yet thou ungratefull cast me off with scorne,
When Heavens purpose raisd your meaner fate.
Oft have I begd for vengeance for this fact,
And with dejected knees, aspiring hands
Have prayd the highest power to inact
The fall of her that on my Trophee stands.
Revenge I have according to my will,
Yet where I wisht this vengeance did not light:
I wisht it should high-hearted *Mariam* kill.
But it against my whilome Lord did fight

With thee sweet Boy I came, and came to try
If thou before his bastards might be plac'd
In *Herods* royall seat and dignitie.

But *Mariams* infants here are onely grac'd,
And now for us there doth no hope remaine:
Yet we will not returne till *Herods* end
Be more confirmed, perchance he is not slaine.
So glorious Fortunes may my Boy attend,
For if he live, hee'll think it doth suffice,
That he to *Doris* shows such crueltie:
For as he did my wretched life dispise,
So doe *I* know I shall despised die.
Let him but prove as naturall to thee,
As cruell to thy miserable mother:
His crueltie shall not upbraided bee
But in thy fortunes. *I* his faults will smother.

Antipat. Each mouth within the Citie loudly cries
That *Herods* death is certaine: therefore wee
Had best some subtill hidden plot devise,
That *Mariams* children might subverted bee,
By poisons drinke, or else by murtherous Knife,
So we may be advanc'd, it skils not how:
They are but Bastards, you were *Herods* wife,
And foule adultery blotteth *Mariams* brow.

Doris. They are too strong to be by us remov'd,
Or else revenges foulest spotted face:
By our detested wrongs might be approv'd,
But weaknesse must to greater power give place.
But let us now retire to grieve alone,
For solitarines best fitteth mone.

Chorus is meant to be Cary

Actus 2. Scœna 4.

Silleus and Constabarus.

Silleus. WEll met *Judean* Lord, the onely wight
Silleus wisht to see. I am to call

Thy tongue to strict account.

Const. For what despight
I ready am to heare, and answere all.
But if directly at the cause *I* gesse
That breeds this challenge, you must pardon me:
And now some other ground of fight professe,
For I have vow'd, vowes must unbroken be.

Sill. What may be your expectation? let me know.

Const. Why? ought concerning *Salom,* my sword
Shall not be welded for a cause so low,
A blow for her my arme will scorne t'afford.

Sill. It is for slandering her unspotted name,
And I will make thee in thy vowes despight,
Sucke up the breath that did my Mistris blame,
And swallow it againe to doe her right.

Const. I prethee give some other quarrell ground
To finde beginning, raile against my name:
Or strike me first, or let some scarlet wound
Inflame my courage, give me words of shame,
Doe thou our *Moses* sacred Lawes disgrace,
Deprave our nation, doe me some despight:
I'm apt enough to fight in any case,
But yet for *Salome* I will not fight.

Sill. Nor I for ought but *Salome*: My sword
That owes his service to her sacred name:
Will not an edge for other cause afford,
In other fight I am not sore of fame.

Const. For her, I pitty thee enough already,
For her, I therefore will not mangle thee:
A woman with a heart so most unsteady,
Will of her selfe sufficient torture bee.

I cannot envy for so light a gaine,
Her minde with such unconstancie doth runne:
As with a word thou didst her love obtaine,
So with a word she will from thee be wonne.
So light as her possesstions for most day
Is her affections lost, to me tis knowne:
As good goe hold the winde as make her stay,
She never loves, but till she call her owne.

She meerly is a painted sepulcher,
That is both faire, and vilely foule at once:
Though on her out-side graces garnish her,
Her mind is fild with worse then rotten bones.
And ever readie lifted is her hand,
To aime destruction at a husbands throat:
For proofes, *Josephus* and my selfe do stand,
Though once on both of us, she seem'd to doat.
Her mouth though serpent-like it never hisses,
Yet like a Serpent, poysons where it kisses.s

Silleus. Well *Hebrew* well, thou bark'st but wilt not bite.

Const. I tell thee still for her I will not fight.

Sille. Why then I call thee coward.

Const. From my heart
I give thee thankes. A cowards hatefull name,
Cannot to valiant mindes a blot impart,
And therefore I with joy receive the same.
Thou know'st I am no coward: thou wert by
At the *Arabian* battaile th'other day:
And saw'st my sword with daring valiancy,
Amongst the faint *Arabians* cut my way.
The blood of foes no more could let it shine,
And twas inameled with some of thine.
But now have at thee, not for *Salome*
I fight: but to discharge a cowards stile:

28

Here gins the fight that shall not parted be,
Before a soule or two indure exile.

Silleus. Thy sword hath made some windowes for my blood,
To shew a horred crimson phisnomie:
To breath for both of us me thinkes twere good,
The day will give us time enough to die

Const. With all my hart take breath, thou shalt have time,
And if thou list, a twelve month, let us end:
Into thy cheekes there doth a palenes clime,
Thou canst not from my sword thy selfe defend.
What needest thou for *Salome* to fight,
Thou hast her, and may'st keepe her, none strives for her:
I willingly to thee resigne my right,
For in my very soule I do abhorre her.

Thou seest that I am fresh, unwounded yet,
Then not for feare I do this offer make:
Thou art with losse of blood, to fight unfit,
For here is one, and there another take.

Silleus. I will not leave as long as breath remaines
Within my wounded body: spare your words,
My heart in bloods stead, courage entertaines,
Salomes love no place for feare affords.

Const. Oh could thy soule but prophesie like mine,
I would not wonder thou should'st long to die:
For *Salome* if I aright divine
Will be then death a greater miserie.

Sille. Then list, Ile breath no longer.

Const. Do thy will,
I hateles fight, and charitably kill. I, I, they fight,
Pittie thy selfe *Silleus*, let not death
Intru'd before his time into thy hart:

Alas it is too late to feare, his breath
Is from his body now about to part,
How far'st thou brave *Arabian*?

Silleus Very well,
My legge is hurt, I can no longer fight:
It onely grieves me, that so soone I fell,
Before faire *Salomes* wrongs I came to right.

Const. Thy wounds are lesse then mortall. Never feare,
Thou shalt a safe and quicke recoverie finde:
Come, I will thee unto my lodging beare,
I hate thy body, but I love thy minde.

Silleus. Thankes noble Jew, I see a courtious foe,
Sterne enmitie to friendship can no art:
Had not my heart and tongue engagde me so,
I would from thee no foe, but friend depart.
My heart to *Salome* is tide so fast,
To leave her love for friendship, yet my skill
Shall be imploy'd to make your favour last,
And I will honour *Constabarus* still.

Const. I ope my bosome to thee, and will take
Thee in, as friend and grieve for thy complaint:
But if we doe not expedition make,
Thy losse of blood I feare will make thee faint.

Chorus.

To heare a tale with eares prejudicate,
It spoiles the judgement, and corrupts the senses.
That humane error given to every state,
Is greater enemie to innocence.
It makes us foolish, heddy, rash, unjust,
It makes us never try before we trust.

It will confound the meaning, change the words,
For it our sence of hearing much deceives
Besides no time to Judgement it affords,
To way the circumstance our eare receives.
The ground of accidents it never tries,
But makes us take for truth ten thousand lies.

Our eares and hearts are apt to hold for good,
That we our selves doe most desire to bee:
And then we drowne objections in the flood
Of partialitie, tis that we see
That makes false rumours long with credit past,
Though they like rumours must conclude at last.

The greatest part of us prejudicate,
With wishing *Herods* death do hold it true:
The being once deluded doth not bate,
The credit to a better likelihood due.
Those few that wish it not the multitude,
Doe carrie headlong, so they doubts conclude.

They not object the weake uncertaine ground,
Whereon they built this tale of *Herods* end:
Whereof the Author scarcely can be found,
And all because their wishes that way bend.
They thinke not of the perill that ensu'th,
If this should prove the contrary to truth.

On this same doubt, on this so light a breath,
They pawne their lives, and fortunes. For they all
Behave them as the newes of *Herods* death,
They did of most undoubted credit call:
But if their actions now doe rightly hit,
Let them commend their fortune, not their wit.

Actus 3. Scœna 1.

Pheroras : Salome

Phero. URge me no more *Graphina* to forsake,
Not twelve howers since I married her for love:
And doe you thinke a sisters power cane mak
A resolute decree, so soone remove?

Salome. Poore minds they are that honour not affects.

Phero: Who hunts for honour, happines neglects.

Salom. You might have bene both of felicitie,
And honour too in equall measure seasde.

Phero: It is not you can tell so well as I,
What tis can make me happie, or displeasde.

Salome. To match for neither beautie nor respects
One meane of birth, but yet of meaner minde,
A woman full of naturall defects,
I wonder what your eye in her could finde.

Phero. Mine eye found loveliness, mine eare found wit,
To please the one, and to enchant the other:
Grace on her eye, mirth on her tongue doth sit,
In lookes a child, in wisedomes house a mother.

Salom. But say you thought her faire, as none thinks else,
Knowes not *Pheroras*, beautie is a blast:
Much like this flower which to day excels,
But longer then a day it will not last.

Phero. Her with exceeds her beautie.

Salo. Wit may show
The way to ill, as well as good you know.

Phero. But wisedome is the porter of her head,
And bares all wicked words from issuing thence.

Sal. But of a porter, better were you sped,
If she against their entrance made defence.

Phero. But wherefore comes the sacred *Ananell,*
That hitherward his hastie steppes doth bend?
Great sacrificer y'are arrived well,
Ill newes from holy mouth I not attend.

Actus 3. Scœna 2.

Pheroras. Salome. Ananell.

Ananell.

MY lippes, my sonne, with peacefull tidings blest,
Shall utter Honey to your listning eare:
A word of death comes not from Priestly brest,
I speake of life: in life there is no feare.
And for the newes I did the Heavens salute,
And fill'd the Temple with my thankfull voice:
For though that mourning may not me pollute,
At pleasing accidents I may rejoyce.

Pheror. Is *Herod* then reviv'd from certaine death?

Sall. What? can your news restore my brothers breath?

Ana. Both so, and so, the King is safe and sound,
And did such grace in royall *Cæsar* meet:
That he with larger stile then ever crownd,

Within this houre Jerusalem will greet.
I did but come to tell you, and must backe
To make preparatives for sacrifice:
I knew his death, your hearts like mine did racke,
Though to conceale it, prov'd you wise.

Salom. How can my joy sufficiently appeare?

Phero. A heavier tale did never pierce mine eare.

Salom. Now *Salome* of happinesse may boast.

Pheror. But now *Pheroras* is in danger most.

Salom. I shall enjoy the comfort of my life.

Pheror. And I shall loose it, loosing of my wife.

Salom. Joy heart, for *Constabarus* shall be slaine.

Phero. Grieve soule, *Graphina* shall from me be tane.

Salom. Smile cheekes, for the faire *Silleus* shall be mine.

Phero. Weepe eyes, for *I* must with a child combine.

Salom. Well brother, cease your mones, on one condition
Ile undertake to winne the Kings consent:
Graphina still shall be in your tuition,
And her with you be nere the lesse content.

Phero. What's the condition? let me quickly know,
That *I* as quickly your command may act:
Were it to see what Hearbs in *Ophir* grow,
Or that the lofty *Tyrus* might be sackt.

Salom. Tis no so hard a taske: It is no more,
But tell the King that *Constabarus* hid

The sonnes of *Baba,* done to death before:
And tis no more then *Constabarus* did.
And tell him more that he for *Herods* sake,
Not able to endure his brothers foe:
Did with a bill our separation make,
Though loth from *Constabarus* else to goe.

Phero. Beleeve this tale for told, Ile goe from hence,
In *Herods* eare the Hebrew to deface:
And I that never studied eloquence,
Doe meane with eloquence this tale to grace. *Exit.*

Salom. This will be *Constabarus* quicke dispatch,
Which from my mouth would lesser credit finde:
Yet shall he not decease without a match,
For *Mariam* shall not linger long behinde.
First Jealousie, if that availe not, feare
Shal be my minister to worke her end;
A common error moves not *Herods* eare,
Which doth so firmly to his *Mariam* bend.
She shall be charged with so horrid crime,
As *Herods* feare shall turne his love to hate:
Ile make some sweare that she desires to clime,
And seekes to poyson him for his estate,
I scorne that she should live my birth t'upbraid,
To call me base and hungry Edomite:

With patient show her choller I betrayd,
And watcht the time to be reveng'd by slite.
Now tongue of mine with scandall load her name,
Turne hers to fountaines, *Herods* eyes to flame:
Yet first I will begin *Pheroras* suite,
That he my earnest businesse may effect:
And I of *Mariam* will keepe me mute,
Till first some other doth her name detect.
Who's there, *Silleus* man? How fares your Lord?
That your aspects doe beare the badge of sorrow?

The Tragedy of Mariam: The Fair Queen of Jewry

Silleus man.

He hath the marks of *Constabarus* sword,
And for a while desires your sight to borrow.

Salom. My heavy curse the hatefull sword pursue,
My heavier curse on the more hatefull arme
That wounded my *Silleus*. But renew
Your tale againe. Hath he no mortall harme?

Silleus man.

No signe of danger doth in him appeare,
Nor are his wounds in place of perill seene:
Hee bides you be assured you need not feare,
He hopes to make you yet *Arabias* Queene.

Salom. Commend my heart to be *Silleus* charge,
Tell him, my brothers suddaine comming now:
Will give my foote no roome to walke at large,
But I will see him yet ere night I vow.

Actus 3. Scœna 3.

Mariam and Sohemus.

Mariam.

SOhemus, tell me what the newes may be
That makes your eyes so full, your cheekes so blew?

Sohem. I know not how to call them. Ill for me
Tis sure they are: not so I hope for you.
Herod

Mari. Oh, what of *Herod*?

36

Sohem. *Herod* lives.

Mari. How! lives? What in some Cave or forrest hid?

Sohem. Nay, backe return'd with honor. *Cæsar* gives
Him greater grace then ere *Anthonius* did.

Mari. Foretell the ruine of my family,
Tell me that I shall see our Citie burnd:
Tell me I shall a death disgracefull die,
But tell me not that *Herod* is returnd.

Sohem. Be not impatient Madam, be but milde,
His love to you againe will soone be bred:

Mar. I will not to his love be reconcilde,
With solemne vowes I have forsworne his Bed.

Sohem. But you must breake those vowes.

Mar. Ile rather breake
The heart of *Mariam.* Cursed is my Fate:
But speake no more to me, in vaine ye speake
To live with him I so profoundly hate.

Sohem. Great Queene, you must to me your pardon give,
Sohemus cannot now your will obey:
If your command should me to silence drive,
It were not to obey, but to betray.
Reject, and slight my speeches, mocke my faith,
Scorne my observance, call my counsell nought:
Though you regard not what *Sohemus* saith,
Yet will *I* ever freely speake my thought.
I feare ere long *I* shall faire *Mariam* see
In wofull state, and by her selfe undone:
Yet for your issues sake more temp'rate bee,
The heart by affabilitie is wonne.

Mari. And must *I* to my Prison turne againe?
Oh, now *I* see *I* was an hypocrite:
I did this morning for his death complaine,
And yet doe mourne, because he lives ere night.
When *I* his death beleev'd, compassion wrought,
And was the stickler twixt my heart and him:
But now that Curtaine's drawne from off my thought,
Hate doth appeare againe with visage grim:
And paints the face of *Herod* in my heart,
In horred colours with detested looke:
Then feare would come, but scorne doth play her part,

And faith that scorne with feare can never brooke.
I know I could inchaine him with a smile:
And lead him captive with a gentle word,
Scorne my looke should ever man beguile,
Or other speech, then meaning to afford.
Else *Salome* in vaine might spend her winde,
In vaine might *Herods* mother whet her tongue:
In vaine had they complotted and combinde,
For I could overthrow them all ere long.
Oh what a shelter is mine innocence,
To shield me from the pangs of inward griefe:
Gainst all mishaps it is my faire defence,
And to my sorrowes yeelds a large reliefe.
To be commandresse of the triple earth,
And sit in safetie from a fall secure:
To have all nations celebrate my birth,
I would not that my spirit were impure.
Let my distressed state unpittied bee,
Mine innocence is hope enough for mee. *Exit.*

Sohem. Poore guiltless Queene. Oh that my wish might place
A little temper now about thy heart:
Unbridled speech is *Mariams* worst disgrace,
And will indanger her without desart.
I am in greater hazard. O're my head,
The fatall axe doth hang unstedily:

My disobediance once discovered,
Will shake it downe: *Sohemus* so shall die.
For when the King shall find, we thought his death
Had bene as certaine as we see his life:
And markes withall *I* slighted so his breath,
As to preserve alive his matchles wife.
Nay more, to give to *Alexanders* hand
The regall dignitie. The soveraigne power,
How I had yeelded up at her command,
The strength of all the citie, *Davids* Tower.
What more then common death may I expect,
Since I too well do know his crueltie:
Twere death, a word of *Herods* to neglect,

What then to doe directly contrarie?
Yet life I quite thee with a willing spirit,
And thinke thou could'st not better be imploi'd:
I forfeit thee for her that more doth merit,
Ten such were better dead then she destroi'd.
But fare thee well chast Queene, well may I see
The darknes palpable, and rivers part:
The sunne stand still. Nay more retorted bee,
But never woman with so pure a heart.
Thine eyes grave majestie keepes all in awe,
And cuts the winges of every loose desire:
Thy brow is table to the modest lawe,
Yet though we dare not love, we may admire.
And if I die, it shall my soule content,
My breath in *Mariams* service shall be spent.

Chorus.

TIs not enough for one that is a wife
To keepe her spotles from an act of ill:
But from suspition she should free her life,
And bare her selfe of power as well as will.
Tis not so glorious for her to be free,
As by her proper selfe restrain'd to bee.

When she hath spatious ground to walke upon,
Why on the ridge should she desire to goe?
It is no glory to forbeare alone,
Those things that may her honour overthrowe.
But tis thanke-worthy, if she will not take
All lawfull liberties for honours sake.

That wife her hand against her fame doth reare,
That more then to her Lord alone will give
A private word to any second eare,
And though she may with reputation live.
Yet though most chast, she doth her glory blot,
And wounds her honour, though she killes it not.

When to their Husbands they themselves doe bind,
Doe they not wholy give themselves away?
Or give they but their body not their mind,
Reserving that though best, for others pray?
No sure, their thoughts no more can be their owne,
And therefore should to none but one be knowne.

Then she usurpes upon anothers right,
That seekes to be by publike language grac't:
And though her thoughts reflect with purest light,
Her mind if not peculiar is not chast.
For in a wife it is no worse to finde,
A common body, then a common minde.

And every mind though free from thought of ill,
That out of glory seekes a worth to show:
When any's eares but one therewith they fill,
Doth in a sort her pureness overthrow.
Now *Mariam* had, (but that to this she bent)
Beene free from feare, as well as innocent.

interesting that the chorus is read from a book

Actus 4: Scœna 1.

Enter Herod and his attendants.

Herod.

HAile happie citie, happie in thy store,
And happy that thy buildings such we see:
More happie in the Temple where w'adore,
But most of all that *Mariam* lives in thee.
Art thou return'd? how fares my *Mariam? Enter Nutio.* [*Nuntio.*]

Nutio. [*Nuntio.*] She's well my Lord, and will anon be here
As you commanded.

Her. Muffle up thy browe,
Thou daies darke taper. *Mariam* will appeare.
And where she shines, we need not thy dimme light,
Oh hast thy steps rare creature, speed thy pace:
And let thy presence make the day more bright,
And cheere the heart of *Herod* with thy face.

It is an age since *I* from *Mariam* went,
Me thinkes our parting was in *Davids* daies:
The houres are so increast by discontent,
Deepe sorrowe, *Joshua* like the season staies:
But when I am with *Mariam,*time runnes on,
Her sight, can make months, minutes, daies of weeke:
An hower is then no sooner come then gon.
When in her face mine eye for wonders seekes.
You world commanding citie, *Europes* grace,
Twice hath my curious eye your streets survai'd,
And I have seene the stature filled place,
That once if not for griefe had bene betrai'd.
I all your *Roman* beauties have beheld,
And seene the showes your *Ediles* did prepare,
I saw the sum of what in you exceld,

41

Yet saw no miracle like *Mariam* rare.
The faire and famous *Livia, Cæsars*love,
The worlds commanding Mistresse did I see:
Whose beauties both the world and *Rome* approve,
Yet *Mariam: Livia,* is not like to thee.
Be patient but a little, while mine eyes
Within your compass limits be contain'd:
That object straight shall your desires suffice,
From which you were so long a while restrain'd.
How wisely *Mariam* doth the time delay,
Least suddaine joy my fence should suffocate:
I am prepar'd, thou needst no longer stay:
Whose there, my *Mariam,* more then happie fate?
Oh no, it is *Pheroras,* welcome Brother,
Now for a while, *I* must my passion smother.

Actus 4: Scœna 2.

Herod. Pheroras.

Pheroras.

ALl health and safetie waite upon my Lord,
And may you long in prosperous fortunes live

With *Rome* commanding *Cæsar,* at accord,
And have all honors that the world can give.

Herod. Oh brother, now thou speakst not from thy hart,
No, thou hast strooke a blow at *Herods* love:
That cannot quickly from my memory part,
Though *Salome* did me to pardon move.
Valiant *Phasaelus,* now to thee farewell,
Thou wert my kinde and honorable brother:
Oh hapless houre, when you selfe stricken fell,
Thou fathers Image, glory of thy mother.

Had I desir'd a greater sute of thee,
Then to withhold thee from a harlots bed,
Thou wouldst have granted it: but now I see
All are not like that in a wombe are bred.
Thou wouldst not, hadst thou heard of *Herods* death,
Have made his buriall time, thy bridall houre:
Thou wouldst with clamours, not with joyfull breath,
Have show'd the newes to be not sweet but soure.

Phero. Phasaelus great worth I know did staine
Pheroras petty valour: but they lie
(Excepting you your selfe) that dare maintaine,
That he did honor *Herod* more then I,
For what I show'd, loves power constraind me show,
And pardon loving faults for *Mariams* sake.

Herod. Mariam, where is she?

Phero. Nay, I do not know,
But absent use of her faire name I make:
You have forgiven greater faults then this,
For *Constabarus* that against you will
Preserv'd the sonnes of *Baba*, lives in blisse,
Though you commanded him the youths to kill.

Herod. Goe, take a present order for his death,
And let those traytors feele the worst of feares:
Now *Salome* will whine to begge his breath,
But Ile be deafe to prayers: and blind to teares.

Phero. He is my Lord from *Salome* divorst,
Though her affection did to leave him grieve:
Yet was she by her love to you inforst,
To leave the man that would your foes relieve.

Herod. Then haste them to their death. I will requite
Thee, gentle *Mariam. Salome, I* meane

The thought of *Mariam* doth so steale my spirit,
My mouth from speech of her I cannot weane. *Exit.*

Actus 4: Scœna 3.

Herod. Mariam.

Herod.

ANd heere she comes indeed: happily met
My best, and deerest halfe: what ailes my deare?
Thou doest the difference certainly forget
Twixt Duskey habits, and a time so cleare.

Mar. My Lord, I suit my garment to my minde,
And there no cheerfull colours can I finde.

Herod. Is this my welcome? have I longd so much
To see my dearest *Mariam* discontent?
What ist that is the cause thy heart to touch?
Oh speake, that I thy sorrow may prevent.
Art thou not *Juries* Queene, and *Herods* too?
Be my Commandres. be my Soveraigne guide:
To be by thee directed I will woo,
For in thy pleasure lies my highest pride.
Or if thou think *Judeas* narrow bound,
Too strict a limit for thy great command:
Thou shalt be Empresse of *Arabia* crownd,
For thou shalt rule, and I will winne the Land.
Ile robbe the holy *Davids* Sepulcher
To give thee wealth, if thou for wealth do care:
Thou shalt have all, they did with him inter,
And I for thee will make the Temple bare.

Mar. I neither have of power nor riches want,
I have enough, nor doe I wish for more:

44

Your offers to my heart no ease can grant,
Except they could my brothers life restore.
No, had you wisht the wretched *Mariam* glad,

Or had your love to her bene truly tide:
Nay, had you not desir'd to make her sad,
My brother nor my Grandsyre had not dide.

Her. Wilt thou beleeve no oathes to cleere thy Lord?
How oft have *I* with execration sworne:
Thou art by me belov'd, by me ador'd,
Yet are my protestations heard with scorne.
Hircanus plotted to deprive my head
Of this long setled honor that I weare:
And therefore *I* did justly doome him dead,
To rid the Realme from perill, me from feare,
Yet I for *Mariams* sake doe so repent
The death of one: whose blood she did inherit:
I wish I had a Kingdomes treasure spent,
So *I* had nere expeld *Hircanus* spirit.
As I affected that same noble youth,
In lasting infamie my name inrole:
If I not mournd his death with heartie truth.
Did I not shew to him my earnest love,
When I to him the Priesthood did restore?
And did for him a living Priest remove,
Which never had bene done but once before.

Mariam. I know that mov'd by importunitie,
You made him Priest, and shortly after die.

Herod. I will not speake, unles to be beleev'd,
This froward humor will not doe you good:
It hath too much already *Herod* griev'd.
To thinke that you on termes of hate have stood.
Yet smile my dearest *Mariam*, doe but smile,
And I will all unkind conceits exile.

Mar. I cannot frame disguise, nor never taught
My face a looke dissenting from my thought.

Herod. By heav'n you vexe me, build not on my love.

Mar. I wil not build on so unstable ground.

Herod. Nought is so fixt, but peevishnes may move.

Mar. Tis better sleightest cause then none were found.

Herod. Be judge your selfe, if ever *Herod* sought
Or would be mov'd a cause of change to finde:

Yet let your looke declare a milder thought,
My heart againe you shall to *Mariam* binde.
How oft did I for you my Mother chide.
Revile my Sister, and my brother rate:
And tell them all my *Mariam* they belide,
Distrust me still, if there be signes of hate.

Actus 4. Scœna 4.

Herod.

WHat hast though here?

Bu. A drinke procuring love,
The Queene desir'd me to deliver it.

Mar. Did *I* : some hatefull practise this will prove,
Yet can it be no worse then Heavens permit.

Herod. Confesse the truth thou wicked instrument,
To her outrageous will, tis passion sure:

Tell true, and thou shalt scape the punishment,
Which if thou doe conceale thou shalt endure.

Bu. I know not, but I doubt it be no lesse,
Long since the hate of you her heart did cease.

Herod. Know'st thou the cause thereof?

Bu. My Lord I gesse,
Sohemus told the tale that did displease.

Herod. Oh heaven! *Sohemus* false! Goe let him die,
Stay not to suffer him to speake a word:
Oh damned villaine, did he falsifie
The oath he swore ev'n of his owne accord?
Now doe I know thy falshood, painted Divill
Thou white Inchantress. Oh thou art so foule,
That Ysop cannot clense thee worst of evill.
A beauteous body hides a loathsome soule,
Your love *Sohemus* mov'd by his affection,
Though he have ever heretofore bene true:
Did blab forsooth, that I did give direction,
If we were put to death to slaughter you.
And you in black revenge attended now
To adde a murther to your breach of vow.

Mar. Is this a dream?

Her. Oh Heaven, that t'were no more,
Ile give my Realme to who can prove it so:

Would I were like any begger poore,
So I for false my *Mariam* did not know.
Foule pith contain'd in the fairest rinde,
That ever grac'd a Cæder. Oh thine eye
Is pure as heaven, but impure thy minde,
And for impuritie shall *Mariam* die.
Why didst thou love *Sohemus?*

Mar. They can tell
That say I lov'd him, *Mariam* saies not so.

Herod. Oh cannot impudence the coales expell,
That for thy love in *Herods* bosome glow?
It is as plaine as water, and deniall
Makes of thy falsehood but a greater triall.
Hast thou beheld thy selfe, and couldst thou staine
So rare perfection: even for love of thee
I doe profoundly hate thee. Wert thou plaine,
Thou shoul'dst the wonder of *Judea* bee.
But oh thou art not. Hell it selfe lies hid
Beneath thy heavenly show. Yet never were thou chast:
Thou might'st exalt, pull downe, command, forbid,
And be above the wheele of fortune plast.
Hadst thou complotted *Herods* massacre,
That so thy sonne a Monarch might be stilde,
Not halfe so grievous such an action were,
As once to thinke, that *Mariam* is defilde.
Bright workmanship of nature sulli'd ore,
With pitched darknes now thine end shall bee:
Thou shalt not live faire fiend to cozen more,
With heavy semblance, as thou cousnedst mee.
Yet must I love thee in diespight of death,
And thou shalt die in the dispight of love:
For neither shall my love prolong thy breath,
Nor shall thy losse of breath my love remove.
I might have seene thy falsehood in thy face,
Where coul'dst thou get thy stares that serv'd for eyes?
Except by theft, and theft is foule disgrace:
This had appear'd before were *Herod* wise,
But I'me a sot, a very sot, no better.
My wisedome long agoe a wandring fell,

Thy face incountring it, my wit did fetter,
And made me for delight my freedome sell,
Give me my heart false creature, tis a wrong.
My guiltless heart should now with thine be slaine:

Thou hadst no right to looke it up so long,
And with usurpers name I *Mariam* staine.

Enter Bu.

Her. Have you design'd *Sohemus* to his end?

Bu. I have my Lord.

Herod. Then call our royall guard
To doe as much for *Mariam*, they offend
Leave ill unblam'd, or good without reward.
Here take her to her death Come back, come backe,
What ment I to deprive the world of light:
To muffle *Jury* in the foulest blacke,
That ever was an opposite to white.
Why wither would you carrie her:

Sould: You bad
We should conduct her to her death my Lord.

Her. Wie sure I did not, *Herod* was not mad,
Why should she feele the furie of the sword?
Oh now the griefe returnes into my heart,
And pulles me peecemeale: love and hate doe fight:
And now hath bove [love] acquir'd the greater part,
Yet now hath hate, affection conquer'd quite.
And therefore beare her hence: and *Hebrew* why
Seize you with Lyons paws the fairest lam
Of all the flocke? She must not, shall not, die,
Without her I most miserable am.
And with her more then most, away, away,
But beare her but to prison, not to death:
And is she gon indeed, stay villaines stay,
Her lookes alone preserv'd your Soveraignes breath.
Well let her goe, but yet she shall not die,
I cannot thinke she ment to poison me:

But certaine tis she liv'd too wantonly,
And therefor shall she never more be free.

Actus 4. Scœna 5.

Bu. FOule villanie, can thy pitchie coloured soule
Permit thine eare to heare her caules doome?
And not inforce thy tongue that tale controule,
That must unjustly bring her to her toome.
Oh *Salome* thou hast thy selfe repaid,
For all the benefits that thou hast done:
Thou art the cause I have the queene betraid,
Thou hast my hart to darkest false-hood wonne.
I am condemn'd, heav'n gave me not my tongue
To slander innocents, to lie, deceive:
To be the hatefull instrument to wrong,
The earth of greatest glory to bereave.
My sinne ascends and doth to heav'n crie,
It is the blackest deed that ever was:
And there doth record it it downe in leaves of brasse.
Oh how my heart doth quake: *Achitophel,*
Thou found a means thy selfe from shame to free:
And sure my soule approves thou didst not well,
All follow some, and I will follow thee.

Actus 4. Scœna 6.

Constabarus, Babus Sonnes, and their guard.

Const. NOw here we step our last, the way to death,
We must not tread this way a second time:
Yet let us resolutely yeeld our breath,
Death is the only ladder, Heav'n to clime.

Babus 1. Sonne. With willing mind I could my selfe resigne,
But yet it grieves me with a griefe untold:
Our death should be accompani'd with thine,
Our friendship we to thee have dearely fold.

Const. Still wilt thou wrong the sacred name of friend?
Then should'st thou never stile it friendship more:
But base mechanicke traffique that doth lend,
Yet will be sure they shall the debt restore.
I could with needlesse complement returne,
Tis for thy ceremonie I could say:
Tis I that made the fire your house to burne,
For but for me she would not you betray.
Had not the damned woman sought mine end,
You had not bene the subject of her hate:
You never did her hatefull minde offend,
Nor could your deaths have freed your nuptiall fate.
Therefore faire friends, though you were still unborne,
Some other subtiltie devisde should bee:
Were by my life, though guiltles should be torne,
Thus have I prov'd, tis you that die for mee.
And therefore should I weakely now lament,
You have but done your duties, friends should die:
Alone their friends disaster to prevent,
Though not compeld by strong necessitie.
But now farewell faire citie, never more
Shall I behold your beautie shining bright:
Farewell of *Jewish* men the worthy store,
But no farewell to any female wight.
You wavering crue: my curse to you I leave,
You had but one to give you any grace:
And you your selves will *Mariams* life bereave,
Your common-wealth doth innocencie chase.
You creatures made to be the humane curse,
You Tygers, Lyonnesses, hungry Beares,
Teare massacring *Hienas*: nay far worse,
For they for pray doe shed their fained teares.
But you will weepe, (you creature crosse to good)

For your unquenched thirst of humane blood:
You were the Angels cast from heav'n for pride,
And still doe keepe your Angels outward show,
But none of you are inly beautifide,
For still your heav'n depriving pride doth grow.

Did not the sinnes of many require a scourge,
Your place on earth had bene by this withstood:
But since a flood no more the world must purge,
You staid in office of a second flood.
You giddy creatures, sowers of debate,
You'll love to day, and for no other cause,
But for you yesterday did deply hate,
You are the wreake of order, breach of lawes.
You best, are foolish, froward, wanton, vaine,
Your worst adulterous, murderous, cunning proude
And *Salome* attends the latter traine,
Or rather he their leader is allowd.
I do the sottishnesse of men bewaile,
That doe with following you inhance your pride:
T'were better that the humane race should faile,
Then be by such a mischiefe multiplide.
Chams servile curse to all your sexe was given,
Because in in Paradise you did offend:
Then doe we not resist the will of Heaven,
When on your willes like servants we attend?
You are to nothing constant but to ill,
You are with nought but wickednesse indude:
You loves are set on nothing but your will,
And thus my censure I of you conclude.
You are the least of goods, the worst of evils,
Your best are worse then men: your worst then divels.

Babus second sonne.

Come let us to our death: are we not blest?
Our death will freedome from these creatures give:
Those trouble quiet sowers of unrest,

And this I vow that had I leave to live,
I would for ever lead a single life,
And never venture on a divellish wife.

Actus 4. Scœna 7.

Herod and Salome.

Herod.

NAy, she shall die. Die quoth you, she shall:
But for the meanes. The meanes! Methinks tis hard
To finde a meanes to murther her withall,
Therefore I am resolv'd she shall be spar'd.

Salm. Why? let her be beheaded.

Her. That were well,
Thinke you that swords are miracles like you:
Her skinne will ev'ry Curtlax edge refell,
And then your enterprise you well may rue.
What if the fierce Arabian notice take,
Of this your wretched weaponlesse estate:
They answere when we bid resistance make,
That *Mariams* skinne their fanchions did rebate.
Beware of this, you make a goodly hand,
If you of weapons doe deprive our Land.

Sal. Why drowne her then.

Herod. Indeed a sweet device,
Why? would not ev'ry River turn her course
Rather then doe her beautie prejudice?
And be reverted to the proper sourse.
So not a drop of water should be found
In all Judeas quondam firtill ground.

Sal. Then let the fire devoure her.

Her. T'will not bee:
Flame is from her deriv'd into my heart:
Thou nursest flame, flame will not murther thee,
My fairest *Mariam*, fullest of desert.

Salom. Then let her live for me.

Herod. Nay, she shall die,
But can you live without her?

Sal.   doubt you that?

Herod. I 'me sure I cannot. I beseech you trie:
I have experience but I know not what.

Salom. How should I try?

Herod. Why let my love be slaine
But if we cannot live without her sight

Youle finde the meanes to make her breathe againe,
Or else you will bereave my comfort quite.

Sal. Oh *I*: I warrant you.

Herod. What is she gone?
And gone to bid the world be overthrowne:
What? is her hearts composure hardest stone?
To what a passe are cruell women growne?
She is return'd already: have you done?
Ist possible you can command so soone?
A creatures heart to quench the flaming Sonne,
Or from the skie to wipe away the Moone.

Sal. If *Mariam* be the Sunne and Moone, it is:
For I already have commanded this.

Her. But have you seene her cheek?

Sal.   A thousand times,

Herod. But did you mark it too?

Sal.   I very well.

Herod. What ist?

Sal. A Crimson bush, that ever limes
The soule whose foresight doth not much excell.

Herod. Send word she shall not dye. Her cheek a bush,
Nay, then *I* see indeed you mark it not.

Sal. Tis very faire, but yet will never blush,
Though foule dishonors do her forehead blot.

Herod. Then let her die, tis very true indeed,
And for this fault alone shall *Mariam* bleed.

Sal. What fault my Lord?

Herod. What fault ist? You that aske:
If you be ignorant *I* know of none.
To call her backe from death shall be your taske,
I'm glad that she for innocent is knowne.
For on the brow of *Mariam* hangs a Fleece,
Whose slenderest twine is strong enough to binde
The hearts of Kings, the pride and shame of *Greece,*
Troy flaming *Helens* not so fairely shinde.

Salom. Tis true indeed, she layes them out for nets,
To catch the hearts that doe not shune a baite:
Tis time to speake: for *Herod* sure forgets
That *Mariams* very tresses hide deceit.

Her. Oh doe they so? nay, then you doe but well,
In sooth I thought it had beene haire:
Nets call you them? Lord, how they doe excell,
I never saw a net that show'd so faire.

But have you heard her speake?

Sal. You know *I* have.

Her. And were you not amaz'd?

Sal. No, not a whit.

Her. Then t'was not her you heard, her life Ile save,
For *Mariam* hath a world amazing wit.

Salo. She speaks a beauteous language, but within
Her heart is false as powder: and her tongue
Doth but allure the auditors to sinne,
And is the instrument to doe you wrong.

Herod. It may be so: nay, tis so: shee's unchaste,
Her mouth will ope to ev'ry strangers eare:
Then let the executioner make haste,
Lest she inchant him, if her words he heare.
Let him be deafe, lest she do him surprise
That shall to free her spirit be assignde:
Yet what boots deafenes if he have his eyes,
Her murthererr must be both deafe and blinde.
For if he see, he needs must see the starres
That shine on eyther side of *Mariams* face:
Whose sweet aspect will terminate the warres,
Wherewith he should a soule so precious chase.
Her eyes can speake, and in their speaking move,
Oft did my heart with reverence receive
The worlds mandates. Pretty tales of love
They utter, which can humane bondage weave.
But shall I let this heavens modell dye?

Which for a small selfe-portraiture she drew:
Her eyes like starres, her forehead like the skie,
She is like Heaven, and must be heavenly true.

Salom. Your thoughts do rave with doating on the Queen,
Her eyes are ebon hewde, and you'll confesse:
A sable starre hath beene but seldome seene,
Then speake of reason more, of *Mariam* lesse.

Herod. Your selfe are held a goodly creature heere,
Yet so unlike my *Mariam* in your shape:
That when to her you have approached neere,
My selfe hath often tane you for an Ape.
And yet you prate of beautie: goe your waies,
You are to her a Sun burnt Blackamore:

Your paintings cannot equall *Mariams* praise,
Her nature is so rich, you are so poore.
Let her be staide from death, for if she die,
We do we know not what to stop her breath:
A world cannot another *Mariam* buy,
Why stay you lingring? countermaund her death.

Salo. Then youle no more remember what hath past,
Sohemus love, and hers shall be forgot:
Tis well in truth: that fault may be her last,
And she may mend, though yet she love you not.

Her. Oh God: tis true. *Sohemus:* earth and heav'n,
Why did you both conspire to make my curst:
In cousning me with showes, and proofes unev'n?
She show'd the best, and yet did prove the worst.
Her show was such, as had our singing king
The holy *David, Mariams* beautie seene:
The *Hittits* had then felt no deadly sting,
Not *Bethsabe* had never bene a Queene.
Or had his sonne the wisest man of men,
Whose fond delight did most consist in change

Beheld her face, he had bene staid agen,
No creature having her, can wish to range.
Had *Asuerus* seene my *Mariams* brow,
The humble *Jewe*, she might have walkt alone:
Her beauteous vertue should have staid below,
Whiles *Mariam* mounted to the Persian throne.
But what availes it all: for in the waight
She is deceitfull, light as vanitie:
Oh she was made for nothing but a bait,
To traine some haples man to miserie.
I am the haples amn that have bene trainde,
To endles bondage, I will see her yet:
Me thinkes I should discerne her if she fainde.
Can humane eyes be dazde by womans wit?
Once more these eyes of mine with hers shall meet,
Before the headsman doe her life bereave:
Shall I for ever part from thee my sweet?
Without the taking of my latest leave.

Salo: You had as good resolve to save her now,
Ile stay her death, tis well determined:
For sure she never more will breake her vow,
Sohemus and *Josephus* both are dead.

Herod. She shall not live, nor will I see her face,
A long heald wound, a second time doth bleed:
With *Joseph* I remember her disgrace,
A shamefull end ensues a shamefull deed.
Oh that I had not cald to minde anew,
The discontent of *Mariams* wavering hart:
Twas you: you foule mouth'd *Ate*, none but you,
That did the thought hereof to me impart.
Hence from my sight, my blacke tormenter hence,
For hadst not thou made *Herod* unsecure:
I had not doubted *Mariams* innocence,
But still had helf her in my heart for pure.

Salo Ile leave you to your passion: tis no time
To purge me now, though of a guiltless crime. *Exit.*

Herod. Destruction take thee: thou hast made my hart
As heavie as revenge, I am so dull,
Methinkes I am not sensible of smart,
Though hiddious horrors at my bosome pull.
My head waies downwards: therefore will I goe
To try if I can sleepe away my woe.

Actus 4. Scœna 8.

Mariam.

AM I the *Mariam* that presum'd so much,
And deem'd my face must needes preserve my breath?
I, I it was that thought my beautie such,
At it alone could countermaund my death.
Now death will teach me: he can pale as well
A cheeke of roses, as a cheeke lesse bright:
And dim an eye whose shine doth most excell,
As soone as one that casts a meaner light.

Had not my selfe against my selfe conspirde,
No plot: no adversarie from without
Could *Herods* love from *Mariam* have retirde,
Or from his heart have thrust my semblamce out.
The wanton *Queene* that never lov'd for love,
False *Cleopatra*, wholly set on gaine:
With all her slights did prove: yet vainly prove,
For her the love of *Herod* to obtaine.
Yet her allurements, all her courtly guile,
Her smiles, her favours, and her smooth deceit
Could not my face from *Herods* minde exile,
But were with him of lesse then little weight.
That face and person that in *Asia* late
For beauties Goddesse *Paphos* Queene was tane:

That face that did captive great *Julius* fate,
That very face that was *Anthonius* bane.
That face that to be *Egipts* pride was borne,
That face that all the world esteem'd so rare:
Did *Herod* hate, despise, neglect, and scorne,
When with the same, he *Mariams* did compare.
This made that I improvidently wrought,
And on the wager even my life did pawne:
Because I thought, and yet but truly thought,
That *Herods* love could not from me be drawne.
But now though out of time, I plainly see
It could be drawne, though never drawne from me:
Had I but with humilitie bene grac'te,
As well as faire I might have prov'd me wise:
But I did thinke because I knew me chaste,
One vertue for a woman, might suffice.
That mind for glory of our sexe might stand,
Wherein humilitie and chastitie
Doth march with equall paces hand in hand,
But one if single seene, who setteth by?
And I had singly one, but tis my joy,
That I was ever innocent, though sower:
And therefore can they but my life destroy,
My Soule is free from adversaries power.   *Enter Doris.*

You Princes great in power, and high in birth,
Be great and high, I envy not your hap:
Your birth must be from dust: your power on earth,
In heav'n shall *Mariam* sit in *Saraes* lap.

Doris. I heav'n, your beautie cannot bring you thither,
Your soule is blacke and spotted, full of sinne:
You in adultry liv'd nine yeare together,
And heav'n will never let adultry in.

Mar: What art thou that doest poore *Mariam* pursue?
Some spirit sent to drive me to dispaire:

Who sees for truth that *Mariam* is untrue,
If faire she be, she is as chaste as faire.

Doris. I am that *Doris* that was once belov'd,
Belov'd by *Herod*: *Herods* lawfull wife:
Twas you that *Doris* from his side remov'd,
And rob'd from me the glory of my life.

Mar. Was that adultry: did not Moses say,
That he that being matcht did deadly hate:
Might by permission put his wife away,
And take a more belov'd to be his mate?

Doris. What did he hate me for: for simple truth?
For bringing beautious babes for love to him:
For riches: noble birth, or tender youth,
Of for no staine did *Doris* honour dim?
Oh tell me *Mariam*, tell me if you knowe,
Which fault of these made *Herod Doris* foe.
These thrice three years have I with hands held up,
And bowed knees fast nailed to the ground:
Besought for thee the dreggs of that same cup,
That cup of wrath that is for sinners found
And now thou are to drinke it: *Doris* curse,
Upon thy selfe did all this while attend,
But now it shall pursue thy children worse.

Mar. Oh *Doris* now to thee my knees I bend,
That hart that never bow'd to thee doth bow:
Curse not mine infants, let it thee suffice,
That Heav'n doth punishment to me allow.
Thy curse is cause that guiltles *Mariam* dies.

Doris. Had I ten thousand tongues, and ev'ry tongue
Inflam'd with poisons power and steept in gall:
My curses would not answere for my wrong,
Though I in cursing thee imployed them all.
Heare thou that didst mount *Gerarim* command,

To be a place whereon with cause to curse:
Stretch thy revenging arme: thrust forth thy hand,
And plague the mother much: the children worse.
Throw flaming fire upon the baseborne heads
That were begotten in unlawful beds.
But let them live till they have sence to know
What tis to be in miserable state:
Then be their neerest friends their overthrow,
Attended be they by suspitious hate.
And *Mariam*, I doe hope this boy of mine
Shall one day come to be the death of thine. *Exit.*

Mariam. Oh! Heaven forbid. I hope the world shall see,
This curse of thine shall be return'd on thee:
Now earth farewell, though I be yet but yong,
Yet *I,* me thinks, have knowne thee too too long. *Exit.*

Chorus.

The fairest action of our humane life,
Is scorning to revenge an injurie:
For who forgives without a further strife,
His adversaries heart to him doth tie.
And tis a firmer conquest truely fed,
To winne the heart, then overthrow the head.

If we a worthy enemie doe finde.
To yeeld to worth, it must be nobly done:
But if of baser mettall be his minde,
In base revenge there is no honor wonne.
Who would a worthy courage overthrow,
And who would wrastle with a worthles foe?

We say our hearts are great and cannot yeeld,
Because they cannot yeeld it proves them poore:
Great hearts are task't beyond their power, but feld
The weakest Lyon will the lowdest roare.
Truths schoole for certaine doth this same allow,

High hartednes doth sometimes teach to bow.

A noble heart doth teach a vertuous scorne,
To scorne to owe a dutie over-long:
To scorne to be for benefits forborne,
To scorne to lie, to scorne to doe a wrong.
To scorne to beare an injurie in minde,
To scorne a free-borne heart slave-like to binde.

But if for wrongs we needs revenge must have,
Then be our vengeance of the noblest kinde:
Doe we his body from our furie save,
And let our hate prevaile against our minde?
What can gainst him a greater vengeance bee,
Then make his foe more worthy farre then hee?

Had *Mariam* scorn'd to leave a due unpaide,
Shee would to *Herod* then have paid her love:
And not have bene by sullen passion swaide
To fixe her thoughts all injurie above
Is vertuous pride. Had *Mariam* thus bene prou'd,
Long famous life to her had bene allowd.

Actus 5. Scœna 1.

Nuntio.

WHen, sweetest friend, did I so farre offend
Your heavenly selfe: that you my fault to quit

Have made me now relator of her end,
The end of beautie? Chastitie and wit,
Was none so haples in the fatall place,
But I, most wretched, for the Queene t'chuse,
Tis certaine I have some ill boding face
That made me culd to tell this luckles newes.
And yet no news to *Herod*: were it new,
To him unhappy t'had not bene at all:
Yet doe I long to come within his vew,
That he may know his wife did guiltles fall:
And heere he comes. Your *Mariam* greets you well.

Enter Herod.

Herod. What? lives my *Mariam*? joy, exceeding joy.
She shall not die.

Nun. Heav'n doth your will repell.

Herod. Oh doe not with thy words my life destroy,
I prethy tell no dying-tale: thine eye
Without thy tongue doth tell but too too much:
Yet let thy tongues addition make me die,
Death welcome, comes to him whose griefe is such.

Nunti. I went amongst the curious gazing troope,
To see the last of her that was the best:
To see if death had hart to make her stoope,

To see the Sunne admiring *Phœnix* next.
When there I came, upon the way *I* saw
The stately *Mariam* not debas'd by feare:
Her looke did seeme to keepe the world in awe,
Yet mildly did her face this fortune beare.

Herod. Thou dost usurpe my right, my tongue was fram'd
To be the instrument of *Mariams* praise:
Yet speake: she cannot be too often fam'd:
All tongues suffice not her sweet name to raise.

Nun. But as she came she *Alexandra* met,

Who did her death (sweet Queene) no whit bewaile,
But as if nature she did quite forget.
She did upon her daughter loudly raile.

Herod. Why stopt you not her mouth? where had she words
To darke that, that Heaven made so bright?
Our sacred tongue no *Epithite* affords,
To call her other then the worlds delight.

Nun. Shee told her that her death was too too good,
And that already she had liv'd too long:
She said, she sham'd to have a part in blood
Of her that did the princely *Herod* wrong.

Herod. Base picke-thanke Divell. Shame, twas all her glory,
That she to noble *Mariam* was the mother:
But never shall it live in any storie
Her name, except to infamy ile smother.
What answere did her princely daughter make?

Nun. She made no answere, but she lookt the while,
As if thereof she scarce did notive take,
Yet smilde, a dutifull, though scornefull smile.

The Tragedy of Mariam: The Fair Queen of Jewry

Her. Sweet creature, I that looke to mind doe call,
Full oft hath *Herod* bene amaz'd withall.

Nun. Go on, she came unmov'd with pleasant grace,
As if to triumph her arrivall were:
In stately habite, and with cheerfull face:
Yet ev'ry eye was moyst, but *Mariams* there.
When justly opposite to me she came,
She pickt me out from all the crue:
She beckned to me, cald me by my name,
For she my name, my birth, and fortune knew.

Herod. What did she name thee? happy, happy man,
Wilt thou not ever love that name the better?
But what sweet tune did this faire dying Swan
Afford thine care: tell all, omit no letter.

Nun. Tell thou my Lord, said she.

Her. Mee, ment she mee?
Ist true, the more my shame: *I* was her Lod,
Were *I* not made her Lord, *I* still should bee:

But now her name must be by me adord.
Oh say, what said she more? each word she sed
Shall be the food whereon my heart is fed.

Nun: Tell thou my Lord thou saw'st me loose my breath.

Herod. Oh that I could that sentence now controule.

Nun. If guiltily eternall be my death,

Her. I hold her chast ev'n in my inmost soule.

Nun. By three daies hence if wishes could revive,
I know himselfe would make me oft alive.

Herod. Three daies: three houres, three minutes, not so much
A minute in a thousand parts divided,
My penitencie for her death is such,
As in the first I wisht she had not died.
But forward in thy tale.

Nun. Why on she went,
And after she some silent praier had sed
She did as if to die she were content,
And thus to heav'n her heav'nly soule is fled.

Herod. But art thou sure there doth no life remaine?
Ist possible my *Mariam* should be dead,
Is there no tricke to make her breathe againe?

Nun. Her body is divided from her head.

Her. Why yet me thinkes there might be found by art,
Strange waies of cure, tis sure rare things are don:
By an inventive head, and willing heart.

Nun. Let not my Lord your fancies idlely run.
It is as possible it should be seene,
That we should make the holy Abraham live,
Though he intomb'd two thousand yeares had bene,
As breath againe to slaughtred *Mariam* give.
But now for more assaults prepare your eares,

Herod. There cannot be a further cause of mone,
This accident shall shelter me from feares:
What can I feare? already *Mariams* gone.
Yet tell ev'n what you will:

Nun. As I came by,
From *Mariams* death I saw upon a tree,
A man that to his necke a cord did tie:

67

Which cord he had designd his end to bee.
When me he once discern'd, he downwards bow'd.
And thus with fearefull voyce she cride alowd,
Goe tell the King he trusted ere he tride,
I am the cause that *Mariam* causeles dide.

Herod. Damnation take him, for it was the slave
That said she ment with poisons deadly force
To end my life that she the Crowne might have:
Which tale did *Mariam* from her selfe divorce.
Oh pardon me thou pure unspotted Ghost,
My punishment must needes sufficient bee,
In missing that content I valued most:
Which was thy admirable face to see.
I had but one inestimable Jewell,
Yet one I had no monarch had the like.
And therefore may I curse my selfe as cruell:
Twas broken by a blowe my selfe did strike.
I gaz'd thereon and never thought me blest,
But when on it my dazled eye might rest:
A pretious Mirror made by wonderous art,
I prized it ten times dearer then my Crowne,
And laide it up fast foulded in my heart:
Yet I in suddaine choler cast it downe.
And pasht it all to peeces: twas no foe,
That robd me of it, no *Arabian* host,
Nor no *Armenian* guide hath usde me so.
But *Herods* wretched selfe hath *Herod* crost.
She was my gracefull moytie, me accurst,
To slay my better halfe and save my worst.
But sure she is not dead you did but jest,
To put me in perplexitie a while,
Twere well indeed if I could so be drest:
I see she is alive, me thinkes you smile.

Nun. If sainted *Abel* yet deceased bee,
Tis certaine *Mariam* is as dead as hee.

The Tragedy of Mariam: The Fair Queen of Jewry

Her. Why then goe call her to me, bid her now

Put on faire habite, stately ornament:
And let no frowne oreshade her smoothest brow,
In her doth *Herod* place his whole content.

Nun. Sheel come in stately weedes to please your sence,
If now she come attirde in robe of heaven:
Remember you your selfe did send her hence,
And now to you she can no more be given.

Herod. Shee's dead, hell take her murderers, she was faire,
Oh what a hand she had, it was so white,
It did the whitenes of the snowe impaire:
I never more shall see so sweet a sight.

Nun. Tis true, her hand was rare.

Herod. her hand? her hands;
She had not singly one of beautie rare,
But such a paire as heere where *Herod* stands,
He dares the world to make to both compare.
Accursed *Salome*, hadst thou bene still.
My *Mariam* had bene breathing by my side:
Oh never had I: had I had my will,
Sent forth command, that *Mariam* should have dide.
But *Salome* thou didst with envy vexe,
To see thy selfe out-matched in thy sexe:
Upon your sexes forehead *Mariam* sat,
To grace you all like an imperiall crowne,
But you fond foole have rudely pusht thereat,
And proudly puld your proper glory downe.
One smile of hers: Nay, not so much a looke
Was worth a hundred thousand such as you,
Judea how canst thou the wretches brooke.
That robd from thee the fairest of the crew?
You dwellers in the now deprived land,
Wherein the matchles *Mariam* was bred:

Why graspe not each of you a sword in hand,
To ay me at me your cruell Soveraignes head.
Oh when you thinke of *Herod* as your King.
And owner of the pride of *Palestine:*
This act to your remembrance likewise bring,

Tis I have overthrowne your royall line.
Within her purer vaines the blood did run,
That from her Grandam *Sara* she deriv'd,
Whose beldame age the love of Kings hath wonne,
Oh that her issue had as long bene li'vd.
But can her eye be made by death obscure?
I cannot thinke but it must sparkle still:
Foule sacriledge to rob those lights so pure,
From out a Temple made by heav'nly skill.
I am the Villaine that have done the deed,
The cruell deed, though by anothers hand,
My word though not my sword made *Mariam* bleed,
Hircanus Grandchild did at my command.
That *Mariam* that I once did love so deare,
The partner of my now detested bed,
Why shine you sun with an aspect so cleare?
I tell you once againe my *Mariams* dead.
You could but shine, if some *Egyptian* blows,
Or *Æthiopian* doudy lose her life:
This was, then wherefore bend you not your brows,
The King of *Juries* fair and spotles wife.
Denie thy beames, and *Moone* refuse thy light,
Let all the starres be darke, let *Juries* eye
No more distinguish which is day and night:
Since her best birth did in her bosome die.
Those fond Idolaters the men of *Greece,*
Maintaine these orbes are safely governed:
That each within themselves have Gods a peece,
By whom their stedfast course is justly led,
But were it so, as so it cannot bee,
They all would put their mourning garments on:
Not one of them would yeeld a light to mee,

To me that is the cause that *Mariams* gon.
For though they fame their *Saturne* melancholy,
Of sowre behaviours, and of angry moode.
They fame him likewise to be just and holy,

And justice needes must seeke revenge for blood.
Their *Jove,* if *Jove* he were, would sure desire.
To punish him that slew so faire a lasse:
For *Ledaes* beautie set his heart on fire,
Yet she not halfe so faire as *Mariam* was.
And *Mars* would deeme his *Venus* had bene slaine,
Sol to recover her would never sticke:
For if he want the power her life to gaine:
Then Physicks God is but an Empericke.
The Queene of love would storme for beauties sake,
And *Hermes* too, since he bestow'd her wit,
The nights pale light for angrie griefe would shake,
To see chast *Mariam* die in age unfit.
But oh I am deceiv'd, she past them all
In every gift, in every propertie:
Her Excellencies wrought her timeless fall,
And they rejoyc'd, not griev'd to see her die.
The *Paphian* Goddesse did repent her wast,
When she to one such beautie did allow:
Mercurius thought her wit his wit surpast,
And *Cinthia* envi'd *Mariams* brighter brow.
But these are ficitons, they are voyd of sence,
The *Greekes* but dreame,and dreaming falsehoods tell:
They neither can offend nor give defence,
And not by them it was my *Mariam* fell.
If she had bene like an *Egiptian* blacke,
And not so faire, she had bene longer livde:
Her overflow of beautie turned backe,
And drownde the spring from whence it was derivde.
Her heav'nly beautie twas that made me thinke
That it with chastitie could never dwell:
But now I see that heavn'n in her did linke,
A spirit and a person to excell.

Ile muffle up my selfe in endles night,
And never let mine eyes behold the light.
Retire thy selfe vile monster, worse then hee

That staind the virgin earth with brothers blood,
Still in some vault or denne inclosed bee,
Where with thy teares thou maist beget a flood,
Which flood in time may drowne thee: happie day
When thou at once shalt die and finde a grave,
A stone upon the vault, some one shall lay,
Which monument shall an inscription have.
And these shall be the words it shall containe,
Heere Herod *lies, that hath his* Mariam *slaine.*

Chorus.

WHo ever hath beheld with steadfast eye,
The strange events of this one onely day:
How many were deceiv'd? How many die,
That once to day did grounds of safetie lay?
It will from them all certaintie bereve,
Since twice six houres so many can deceive.

This morning *Herod* held for surely dead.
And all the *Jewes* on *Mariam* did attend:
And *Constabarus* rise from *Saloms* bed,
And neither dreamd of a divorce or end.
Pheroras joyd that he might have his wife,
And *Babus* sonnes for safetie of their life.

To night our *Herod* doth alive remaine.
The guiltles *Mariam* is depriv'd of breath:
Stout *Constabarus* both divorst and slaine,
The valiant sonnes of *Baba* have their death.
Pheroras sure his love to be bereft,
If *Salome* her sute unmade had left.

Herod this morning did expect with joy.
To see his *Mariams* much beloved face:
And yet ere night he did her life destroy,

And surely thought she did her name disgrace.
Yet now againe so short do humors last,
He both repents her death and knowes her chast.

Had he with wisdome now her death delaide,
He at his pleasure might command her death:
But now he hath his power so much betraide,
As all his woes cannot restore her breath.
Now doth he strangely lunatickly rave,
Because his *Mariams* life he cannot save.

This daies events were certainly ordainde,
To be the warning to posteritie:
So many changes are therein containde,
So admirablie strange varietie.
This day alone, our sagest *Hebrewes* shall
In after times the schoole of wisedome call.

FINIS.

Lightning Source UK Ltd.
Milton Keynes UK
UKHW012004060921
390129UK00002B/559